# *Where Snowflakes Dwindle*

Hannah Scheffler

PublishAmerica
Baltimore

© 2009 by Hannah Scheffler.
All rights reserved. No part of this book may be reproduced, stored in a retrieval system or transmitted in any form or by any means without the prior written permission of the publishers, except by a reviewer who may quote brief passages in a review to be printed in a newspaper, magazine or journal.

First printing

PublishAmerica has allowed this work to remain exactly as the author intended, verbatim, without editorial input.

ISBN: 978-1-61546-566-8 (softcover)
ISBN: 978-1-4489-1876-8 (hardcover)
PUBLISHED BY PUBLISHAMERICA, LLLP
www.publishamerica.com
Baltimore

Printed in the United States of America

To the bestest brudder and Tab ever invented!!

## *A Fool Am I*

An ego boost,
felt so damn used,
the way you'd hold me tight
as lovers 'neath the night.
Never meant to hurt me…
Or so you say,
why was it so easy,
for you to turn away?
You claimed that I lied,
yet you never tried,
to understand,
us at hand.
I hope you cried,
when you said goodbye,
though you came in vain,
I pray, you felt my pain!
I dance with my own drum beat
Who's to say I'm wrong?
You used me,
then confused me,
you strung me along,
swaying me with sweet songs.
Thought there, I belonged

died within you,
cried without you,
curse the ways you led me on!
Silly…pathetic little girl…
Living absent her own world,
wanting a king to stand beside,
yet all is lost amidst the pride.
Who knows if you'll ever see,
the way you truly felt to me,
a mistake it seems,
pleading you not to leave.
I hope you cried when you walked away,
hope you felt the pain I've known,
hope the moment you left something whispered,
'Now YOU'RE all alone.'
You waltzed around assuming,
never stopping to ask why,
following arrogant thoughts,
living your own lie.
If you had all the pieces to build this,
you might finally see,
then you get past the look,
the age,
the destination…
I'm only me.

## A Game of Death

I know you, Death.
You watch me through wool,
sitting disdainfully on a stake ridden throne.
I am familiar with your game…

I saw you excise my eyes,
swallowing them whole,
letting them roll about like dice
in your abdomen…

Death, I can still see.

I heard you hack my ears,
clasping them between thumb and index,
dangling them in a taunting manner,
in front of the hollow cavities that
held my eyes…

Death, I can still hear.

I felt you slash my hands,
again and again,
until they plunged to the floor.

You mockingly placed them,
over the apertures that were once,
my ears…

Death, I can still feel.

I tasted the scalpel
as you severed my tongue,
grasping it tightly and wrapping it
around my blood soaked limbs,
bounding them together…

Death, I can still speak.

I smelled the flames,
as you slowly singed my nose,
gathering the ashes,
sprinkling them in my mouth,
as if to suggest a cure for the pain…

Death, I can still smell your vile stench.

I sensed the frustrations,
as your twisted games could not prevail.
Clever, yet foolish you were,
hindering your purpose and rendering my verses.

I will, however, be whole
you see,
because, Death…

You shall never reach the soul in me.

## *A Lover's Tale*

His sleepy whisper,
as the hours spin,
a warm shadow,
caresses her skin.
Her weary eyes,
close to rest,
a soft breath,
seeks her breasts.
Gentle wind blows,
rustling her hair,
as his fingers trail,
her body bare.
A golden child,
seeks his prey,
finds a lover,
and last they lay.

## *A Moment of Rest*

If a moment could pass,
without a memory,
time would miss,
darkness would fall,
glazed over eyes of all.
No instant could see,
for death would steal light,
and guide it to heaven,
to set it free.
Should this luminance be so divine,
it may never return,
giving the moment no place to live?
Time would cease to exist,
all beings would stand still,
unable to feel a thing,
dwelling endlessly…
in history.

## *Ace of Hearts*

You say you love me,
I see it in your gaze,
you're thinking of her,
each time you look away.
Things have changed,
Your touch feels lost,
hollow and forced,
all at what cost?
You claim to be happy,
content where we stand
poker faces don't lie,
dissatisfied with your hand.
There's beauty with high aces,
her eyes fixated on yours,
with only one glance,
you'll desire more.
I beg and plead for comfort,
commitment and trust,
trying to hold onto,
what became of us.
Instead you glisten,
when you speak her name,
I shouldn't be so jealous,

but I can't be to blame.
Who knows what will happen,
in the next week or two,
when you realize what you have,
and leave me...
for you.

## Addict of Him

The purpose unbeknownst.

Why come back
day after day
to sober kisses,
and drunken love?

What draws one near,
thus erasing the past,
affected by every taste,
impaling the trembling body,
thawing all fibers of being?

What frustrations become of us
melting away with every sweat bead,
why come to him
time after time…
again and again…

Only conclusion,
Is…
Pure addiction.

## *Ailment*

Replacing displacement
reliving this moment
again to my torment
against my enlistment
forever they toss
forgoing my loss
not choosing the boss
unknowing the cross
curse crazed pride
craving to feel alive
paying to ride
praying to die.

## *Alas*

Alas my love, come home
to my dear heart.
On go to a glow,
rove through the start.
A hundred goodbyes,
can never reach to.
Life is but a dream,
that we must go through.
Yesterday was darkened hope,
lasted all night long,
I dreamt I could find him,
thus he was gone.
To come is to leave,
with memory to hold,
I knew no more,
with his tale untold.

## *Amidst the Willows*

Whispering willows tell the tales,
of vexed woods and cursing trails,
her watchful eyes saw the light,
while taunting woods of fearful spite.

Her innocent mind she hid from day,
her famished heart searched the way,
adorned in pain each step she took,
she cried to heavens from her holy book.

She soon found herself, that light,
a thousand moons had near passed by,
she had stolen and tasted morel,
and it poisoned her eyes as she fell.

Willows quietly whisper her tale,
to warn a vex from traveler's trails.

## *An Aimless Wander*

So shiver me timbers,
and sliver me quick,
I shall no longer jump,
O'er that flame burning stick.

For it burneth my fingers,
and it burneth my toes,
as the rage burning flames,
rush through my nose.

No longer shall I be down,
but grown with full strength,
and no rage of any kind,
shall keep at my length.

No rivers of tears,
from my eyes to my feet,
Shall keep me from bread,
I will sing, I will eat.

And poor little chicken,
was wrong with a sigh,
for what was falling,
was not cloud nor sky.

If I jumpeth o'er the moon,
Or ran a great mile,
neither fear nor forks,
shall keep of my smile.

Nothing shall make me down,
nothing shall knock me break,
but kissing that flame,
I shall swim the great lake.

Shallow are the waters,
Deep blue is the lay,
but candlestick nor sky,
shall keep me at bay.

## *Away with Us*

Take me away,
to our special place…
Gaze into my eyes,
transcend the love onto my face.
Torrents of rain,
Crashing—
—thrashing at my sill,
drowning the moans…
the groans,
my body purrs to your gentle strokes.
Take me away
to our secret place…
Reach into my soul,
feel the wine of my taste.
Lighting strikes the skies of war,
suffocating our sweat,
The first moment we met.
our bodies became one,
'neath the slumbering sun.
Take me away,
to our special place…
Where lovers taunt the nights,
let our love, at last, take flight.

## *Beauty in You*

I want to make love to your mind,
our thoughts to intertwine,
to feel you speak through me,
caressing my verbs in sweet harmony.
I want to become your lyrical muse,
waltzing on colors of yellow and rouge,
you to write me as though I were a story,
plaguing my beauty in all of your glory.
In the end, I'm all you'll find,
I want to make love to your mind.

## *Beings of Ashes*

Boring mortals
suffocating dreams
standing still in oblivion.

Ugly taunted creatures
of day—
of night—
floating down rivers
unseen and lifeless
the creeps of a hidden walk
senseless motions.

Hear them speak
of yore unraveled in relations
cryptic tales of evils.

Pathetic beings
of those who stepped a path before
dreamless sensations.

Will these revelations ever become
or burn by fire
and let lay in my bowl of ashes.

You shall die by my hand today.

## Bitter Chase

I beg you to deny me once more,
thrill, I feel to pursue you again,
rush, I rave to sense rejection,
chase a shadow in the midst of a dream.
I see a silhouette of shattered hope,
my faith in you is bare,
you turn and walk further away,
leaving behind a trace of settled dust.
What beauty do you search?
What cause do you yearn?
I can no longer carry your empty words,
that weigh heavy on my skull.
Deny me once more,
let us both roam free,
pointless in misery.
I will leave…
deny me once more.

## *Black Beauty*

Blindness
Entwining and turning—
Lamenting in endless slumber
my only shelter from agony
and hopelessness.

Screaming!
Taunting…
Incensed and deranged—
all
in
ALL
…dead.

## Black Thorn Heart

If the world turned to gray,
would you still have color on your face?
Would you be ok, enough
to set the record straight?
If the dark clouds came to you,
would you know what to say?
Would you be ok, enough
to run…
…run away?
When you depict
the story-line,
do you stand tall
and see all, divine?
You capture pieces,
photos stand still,
enough to freeze up,
your tormented will.
But who's to blame?
"Not I," you claim.
Would it be justice to see you burning,
all your glory,
ashes turning?
If the world disappeared,

would you still have color on your face?
Would you be ok, enough
to just run…
…run away?

## Break

Life seems so bedraggled,
worn, stale, and unclear,
this illimitable self of elegant humor,
senseless of anything shear.
I shed feelings of abandonment,
envision sights of pleasure,
but a stray too far, to fetch,
clasping faith,
as dying without measure.

## *Breaking Yesterday*

Today you lost,
the tomorrow you wanted.
Nobody's perfect,
but who do you know?

Can't buy the odds,
even with prayers.
Nobody cares,
no one has time.

So plead your pity,
breed your vanity,
can't fight this battle,
though you still try.

When life ends,
what will you remember?
You'll never depend on
the ghost of your lies.

When you break,
like shattered panes of glass,
do you fall forward,
retracing your past?

There's a blackened revenge,
against your tired harmony.
Nobody cares,
no one has time.

But you still hate,
That yesterday.
You fall asleep,
And run away.

The hour glass,
Is half past full.
Yet you still fear,
you outlandish fool!

So plead your pity,
breed your vanity,
you can't fight this battle,
and yet you still try.
When your life ends,
what will you remember?
You'll never depend on
the ghost of your lies.

## Broken Eve

Tears fill my eyes,
for I am bound to your love,
By what grace was able to sustain,
misery toils, upon the mention of your name.
Regretting the choices,
While I recollect our past,
I suffer from love chronicles,
heart adorned with lace, has shattered.
The wind tousles the long hair you once worshipped,
and brushes away the tears you once kissed.
Never shall you be seen by these eyes,
I now sanction those eyes to look to others in comfort.
Having lost all hope in you,
I place it now upon these very hands,
restoring my heart once more,
I'll remember you only when I sleep.

## Ceremony of Lovers

An eternity of bliss,
textbook style,
a touch that chills my fruits.

Erotic…

Exotic…

Each spinning hour
You…

You are my euphoria,
tempting kisses,
forbidden secrets,
of your wings woven from sheets,
lips like the sway of the ocean.

We are the horizon
Never ending.
Always moving.

You are my eternity of bliss.

## *Cherubs*

Outlawed from Heaven,
on vertical pleasures,
two cherubs played a tune,
of a duets treasure.

Guilty of the sunsets,
a jealous horizon of stares,
two cherubs played a dance,
solemnly they pair.

An instant of desire,
a moment of release,
two cherubs play a drum,
when the sun lay in peace.

Forbidden from perfection,
a night to last on,
whispers of a story,
as two cherubs played a song.

# *Confused*

Does he love me?
Does he not?
The peddles fall,
creating a plot.

If he does,
I'm in love.
If he's not,
heart breaks, thereof.

Shall I call him?
Shall I wait?
Is he troubled?
Am I, too late?

Thoughts confound…
Does he know?
Words uncertain…
Does it show?

My prayers flow,
to Him above,
guess I'm unsure,
about this thing, called love.

## *Counting My Times*

How many times can you tear me apart,
before you destroy my humble heart?
How many tears must I cry
before my withering soul takes flight?
How many nights must I stay awake,
before my weary eyes take break?
When will you understand,
that I can no longer raise my hand?
No more can I praise your stance,
I can no longer hold it to chance.
How many trials must I prove,
that my entire being belongs with you?
When the future of 'us' is slowly mounting,
baby, can you hear me counting?

## *Crest of Lies*

The savory essence,
of blazing crescents,
inspires a soul,
to finally take toll.

To stir up the ashes,
of the maddening masses,
spreading 'cross the sky,
caging the sly.

Your moment has come,
to dwell the undone,
place out your hand,
take on your brand.

Such grave seeking wisdom,
we'll certainly see,
should you kneel down,
and set your lies free.

## *Dead Writing*

Bitterly sweet,
sweetly divine,
sweating the ocean,
losing my mind.
Running in slow,
shooting my pain,
being reborn,
remaining restrained.
Holding my breath,
hugging a pail,
releasing sickness,
brain's gone stale.
Falling in love,
with visions unreal,
tasting tears,
losing feel.
Sitting up slowly,
begin to recline,
'cause I'm bitterly sweet,
and sweetly divine.

## Dear Husband of Mine

Oh husband of mine,
you fret for the worst,
marriage is bliss,
my love is no curse.

Sweet husband of mine,
no lies can I tell,
this union is real,
I cast you no spell.

Darling husband of mine,
I give you my heart,
vows will hold true,
from you I won't part.

Dear husband of mine,
I sit at your grave,
properly placed,
I am your slave.

Beloved husband of mine,
I'm forever in woe,
they say to move on,
but what do they know?

## *Dear, You*

I feel you…
I bleed you…
You see me as dead.

I love you…
Despise you…
Yet it's all in my head.

When will you…
Release me…
From this troubled stance?

Walk away, you…
I'm ok…
Just lost in this trance.

When will you see…
When will it lead…
To you.

I cry out in vain…
Concealing the pain…
From you.

I crave you…
But fear you…
As you beat on my pride.

Raping…
Repenting…
You push me aside.

The whispers…
The taunting…
Please throw me away.

I need you…
I love you…
But not on this day.

## *Denied to Heaven*

The Hell inside
poured out of my eyes
before me, a beast, stood.
Darkness around paced beneath my skin.
My soul withered as I kissed death
with blood stained lips and drank of its glory.
I lusted over its masculine figure.
It stared into my eyes, and—
—placed its tongue deep within my body.
I knew it could taste my insecurity and fear.
God warned that bare faith would only bring darkness.
Here stood, I, making love to—
demise, evils of the world who danced around me
hissed, giggled, and chanted their threats.
My skin was set aflame, the pain struck down.
Death laughed as my body blistered, tearing apart.
So alive, I could be.
So innocent, I would have been—
Had I not denied myself to Heaven…

## Desperate Housewife

In a time of despair as begin to repair, the lost and lonely that becomes me,
in truth I am known, though much is unknown, on where I'm supposed to be.
I clinch my right fist; I am totally pissed, to be damaged by those worthy I once thought,
I beg me a prayer, to peel off a layer, and reveal for what I once fought.
I hang on a wire, of a desperate desire, to feel what I did once before,
I see all my loves, rip off my gloves, I am now…
Forever…
Shutting that door.

## *Donor*

Reliving my pain,
again and again,
the beauty of my womb,
becoming consumed.
Turning immune
to the absence of my heart,
Growing away,
cultivating my pain,
missing, dear sweet yesterday.
The beauty of my body,
bearing the pieces of her father,
as she moves further,
from her necessities.
Wondering if she appreciates me,
knowing she will forgive me,
when she no longer shows me.
Reliving my pain,
again and again,
the beauty of my womb.

## *Downtime*

How many times,
have I lost my mind,
I'm just downtime, baby,
just your downtime.

Mumbling in parables,
you don't understand,
when asking cue questions,
why not raise your hand?

Trivial in monogamy,
Can't possibly know me,
just downtime, baby,
holding hopes of maybe.

Clue me in, on your plans,
inch me into your heart,
give me something to go on,
I don't want to grow apart.

Kiss me without warning,
take me by the hand,
want me when I'm near,
and love me because you can.

## *Dream Lover*

As I stared into his dark brown eyes,
and ran my fingers by his sides,
his gentle lips pressed onto mine,
and I knew with a song, it was a sign.

He told me once with a bliss,
but never did he say it like this.

Come close and be mine, my love.
Live with me here and above.

He became a blur, as my heart was broken,
For that moment, I had awoken.

## *Enchantment*

Boredom stricken gulls,
fly about my wing,
golden fairies fly,
apt to interest me.

Conforming lonely sways,
creep up wildly,
waiting my return,
shadowed pleasantly.

Waving time around,
spent into a breeze,
a dragon's fierce desire,
wanting stars to please.

Dancing on the moon,
blankly seeking me,
motions blown away,
kissed off silently.

## *Epics of Era*

As the mystic rain adorns the earth,
the sun has set for a starlit birth,
the sky lays low and red to warn,
the sailor's calm was not yet born.

An eerie crescent does wake the night,
while dove's sweet songs, at last, take flight,
a holy reign skilled not the power,
softly nestled in our lasting hour.

Streams of hope sleep far away,
And the mind's sweet songs break through 'til day.

## Escape This Drug

Blackness...

Taunting...

Ripping within my soul.

Take another hit,
as poisonous gases carry wrath,
upon my brain.

Spirits dancing round...
what a jolly round they sway.

Impale a little deeper,
as it takes all your troubles away.

Crash...

Collide into my core,
where no resistance shall follow.

Be gone...

Awaken suddenly!

Mom is on the phone
Hurry! Yes, yes. I'm well mother…'

Sweet drug,
bleed into my spirit,
just a little more.

Float away silently.

I'm gone…

So long…

Goodbye.

## Eternal Remnants of Silence

What's the point of spoken words?
A deaf world cares not to listen,
written scripts merely pass the time,
screaming the sorrows dwelling within,
echoing about inside a mind,
until they're plucked for inspiration,
to write another unheard tale,
serving only as my journal's companion,
unseen, unheard, silent, and still,
expressions lost in translation,
hidden, useless, hushed, and calm,
until someone finally cares to hear them.

## *Every Night*

I can still feel,
your touch embrace me softly,
every night since,
I imagined that you love me.
I can still taste,
the sweet sugar of your lips,
every night since,
I imagined our first kiss.

Come speak to me,
I hear your mind is screaming,
come sneak away,
and hush the worlds refuse.
We'll dance along,
the whispers of the sunset,
my lips are sweet,
so long as they kiss you.

I want to know,
every crevice of your body,
every day since,
I let my wild heart run free.
I want to love,

every moment in your life,
spend every day,
with you standing by my side.

I missed out on the good times,
making nothing of my old rhymes,
wonder who would ever read me,
care to care and actually see me.

So, come speak to me,
I hear your soul is screaming,
come sneak away,
and hush the worlds refuse.
We'll dance along,
the whispers of the moonlight,
my lips are sweet,
so long as they kiss you.

## *Fall Away*

When you hit me,
I feel it!
When you hurt me,
I reveal it!
When I yell back,
You hate it!
When you want forgiveness,
I debate it!
When you control me,
I know it!
When I make money,
You blow it!
When I need love,
You make it!
When you want more,
I fake it!
When we're together,
I save it!
When we're apart,
I crave it!
When we have problems,
You live it!
When you need help,

I give it!
When you slam doors,
I hear it!
When you return,
I fear it!

## *Fin*

Memoirs gently written,
to those who softly speak them.
To whom they will be given,
of pasts they will relive.
Who writes such scripts of yore,
That many followers, solemnly adore?
What of creating a ribbon,
that cascades upon them?
For where they have been driven,
these pasts they now envision…

## *Fluid*

Red ocean of blood,
sweet river of fear,
come to me,
feel me,
see me here.

I cry your waters,
breathe your sorrow,
join me now,
taste my lips,
over me you reign.

Deep sea of passion,
great lake of yore,
may the past be broken,
the future be death,
everlasting in you I'll soar.

## For Whom the Trumpet Solemnly Plays

For whom the twilight withers away,
in tow, a tale pursues,
vowing in death, a silent prayer
a toll this oath subdues.

For where this fallen hero lies,
the ground adjourns undone,
declaring peace for grieving kin,
as tears liquefy the sun.

## Forever's Tomorrow

I promise you a first tomorrow,
to be true.

I promise you a second tomorrow,
I'll love you.

I promise you a third tomorrow,
I'll be there.

I promise you a fourth tomorrow,
and that I'll care.

I promise you a fifth tomorrow,
and five tomorrows after then.

I promise an eleventh tomorrow,
sweet kisses over and again.

I promise you a twelfth tomorrow,
as long as the open sky.

I promise you all the tomorrows I have,
until the day I die.

## Free from Love

I wish I could love you,
the way you love me,
the way you are.

I wish that I adored you,
The way I used to,
So long ago.

Things are changing,
I'm going places,
I've never been before.

My dreams are right within my reach,
I feel them
Closer to my door.

I don't know,
Not yet—
Where you fit in here.

I wish that things were simple,
the way they once were,
so fancy free.

I wish I could get over,
the way my heart broke,
the day you left me.

Bear with me.
I am trying,
moving, changing.

I believe I will be free,
when you finally
stop chasing me.

## *Glass Box*

They stand,
no one talks
not even a nod,
in my world they barely exist,
in their precious glass houses.

I peek inside,
They X-Ray me,
unleashed,
unheard,
cast out from their containment,
unable to relate.

My payment?
…Time…
it stirs by,
my own is no longer to be wasted.

Look at them
Can't you see them—
unable to comprehend what lies beyond them—
dancing on clouds of ignorance—
like a plethora of birds running into windows?

Please…
I beg you…

Pardon me for laughing…

## *Haste Hidden*

Can't find my mind,
hit rewind n' intertwine.
With my soul I feel whole,
play a role with fair and drole.
I'm whipped,
stripped,
n' tripped,
fed unto the dead,
Covered in red, t'has been said,
I'm told my hard work's sold.
My heart gold, yet weary n' old,
I lay to rest n' cover my chest
with sands of earth…
…awaiting rebirth.

## *I See Through You*

You preserve me in a home,
I struggle to call my own.
Your freedom based philosophies
are contrary to reality.
You strive to comfort me
by your inventive tales.
Why so, might I ask,
do you bare the horrors of your past?
You conceal its impact with synthetic smiles.
A mere glimpse or gaze…
I see through my blindness.

## *I Wanna Write a Poem*

I wanna write a poem,
but I haven't been inspired.
I wanna write a poem,
but I haven't a desire.
I wanna write a poem,
but my mind just can't think.
I wanna write a poem,
but my thoughts just won't link.
I wanna write a poem,
but empty is my heart.
I wanna write a poem,
but I don't know where to start.

## Inside These Eyes

I lay back and close my eyes,
the world is my massage,
I'm reserved in respect,
as I relax and reflect.

Among others I seem real,
I'm here, well put together,
alone I can descramble,
weaken in my babble.

Love me if you must,
though I tarnish the silver lining,
believe what seems unheard of,
because I see with inner eyes.

Confusion is my comfort,
I gather where the questions lie,
speaking in riddles,
desperately trying to rhyme.

## *Intrusion*

He preaches like he knows my name,
with wool-covered eyes he sees,
I'm falling out of love with him,
who's falling more in love with me.
Abuse and love seep through his lips,
how dare he say we're meant to be,
I feel the haunted tone he lives,
how dare he know my destiny.

## *Justin*

You'll never feel the way
I felt that day.
You'll never understand
the way I pay.
You'll never see the lies behind those eyes,
or the way I sit at night and cry.
I felt your nimble touch,
your starving crutch,
my moans were too much,
they flew through me,
like destiny on ebony playing within me.
I allow silence dwell like hell in my soul,
playing your role,
I paid the toll.
Overdosed in a rose,
covered by the clothes,
you ripped as I tripped over the bed,
with the tip of your head,
you left me for dead,
crippled by fear,
tasting my tears,
though there are years between us.
Betrayed by trust for lust you tested,

the things I bet for thee,
only wanting to be free.
You'll never know the pain,
the way I strain.
Day by rainy day…
I will always pay.

## Kingdom of Me

I am a fortress,
bow to my despair.
I wander through you,
as I build my temples.
I am a masterpiece of your hidden desires,
the quest to be known.
On a hill you wait,
the higher you climb.
The deeper I seek,
as you play me your song,
I will travel to your harbor.
I am love.
I am hate.
I will be your carriage,
let go of your rope,
so I can carry you to the roads I have built,
and guide you to my village.
For…
I am your queen,
and you are my kingdom.

## *Last Breath*

Lost in mystic fog
I scurry about
like a small ant
searching for the ground.

I bear the tears
of a thousand widows
for I am lost
with nowhere to go.

I sense, death is near
while I shiver in a breeze
this is my last morn, I fear
as it whispers through the trees.

I'm apt to fall,
and never awake
'Tis through this fog
my body will break.

No need for goodbyes
there's no one around
everyone's vanished
without a sound.

The rocks cave in
the trap was set
closing my eyes
at last, I rest.

## *Liquefied*

Crimson ocean of blood,
sweet river of fear,
come to me,
feel me,
see me here.

I cry your streams,
breathe your sorrows,
join me now,
taste my lips,
over me, you reign.

Deep sea of passion,
great lake of yore,
may the past be broken,
the future be death,
everlasting in you, I'll soar.

## *Losing Connection*

I see the silhouette of a tainted past,
no true shape withholding its organs,
no genuine color expressing the origin.
An outline of yore,
somehow able to combine memories,
while erasing thoughts.
The skew timelines connect the pieces,
some of which...
I once chose to forget.
Portraits play like long forgotten cinema,
yet, the reels keep coming loose.
When a past is remembered,
yet felt-less,
does it simply reside as a plane of...
nothingness?

## *Love Away!*

Would it be cliché to say
that you melt my sorrows away?
When the night is gray,
you bring forth the day.
Can I say, that I pray,
to kiss your lips everyday?
I wish to convey,
the very way,
you make me feel,
you are my bay,
when I stumble astray.
Have you heard,
these words,
before?
Would it be too cliché to say,
that you take my breath away?

## *Making Me*

Clever that tone that whispered in my ear
fixated on me
he was a fixation like death to suffocation
like the christening moon
on the crest of the ocean
his touch swayed me into euphoria
unknown to any drug.
I was a pearl…
Hidden.
dancing in the sugary lips beneath the stars.
He cradled my body.
Gripped my soul.
Left me breathless amidst dreams.

## *Masked Dimensions*

I breed vain into the world of hostile illusions,
vexed, wearing no amulet,
the savage humanity grows lost around me,
as I wilt into the dawn of tomorrow.
My words are of complete delicacy,
and yet they wait,
as I do,
for a moment.
I sit with those in strange postures,
searching for perfection,
a quilted attire seems to overcome their trance expressions,
as a disconsolate melody impels the weakened souls to a harmonic echo,
and shuffles the mind of an everlasting obsession.
To entertain an absent peace of complete delusion,
seems...
adrift with the wake.
I know not, for I seek not,
the days of our absence have long passed away.

## *Merlot*

Oh sweet wine
savoring my lips,
as I sip your vine.
You inspire,
thoughts I would
normally retire.
I recall,
lingering nights,
and crazed flights.
You move me,
to speak the silence,
against the violence.
You soothe me,
As I arduously define,
line by line.
You release me,
swaying my verbs,
in ecstasy.

Oh sweet—
—Sweet wine…

## *Miss the Rain*

If I could miss the rain,
I'll do just fine.
If I could miss the rain,
I wouldn't lose my mind.
That starving rain,
beats hard upon my skull,
the deepened pain,
the rain will fall.
If I could miss the rain,
and escape it miseries,
If I could miss the rain,
I'd be able to see.
If I could miss the rain,
that falls dead from the sky,
If I could miss the rain,
I would finally stay dry.

## Night's Slave

The herod spoke a tale of yore
Once sought a dream to soar

The grave unspoken
My smile has yet been broken

The iridescent soften charm
Simmers out naturalistic harm

Glazed across a starlit moon
Leaving space in sinful gloom

I choose to seek a different course
Bathing you with my remorse

Future filters out my mind
Leaving you left behind

Upon an open grave
You are now night's slave

## *Nomad*

Mellow roaming quilts the soul,
while drifting ships keep a toll.

Merry gardens sway in tune,
while the sun's rays sprinkle June.

Cooling weather may seem fright,
yet sitting by fire, quiets the night.

Midday breezes swing the leaves,
frantic water, while ocean heaves.

Chanting threats of tearful hopes,
while praying, builds golden ropes.

## Nothing to Spare

Heart beats—
Can anyone hear them?
Eyes bleed—
can anyone see them?
breath gasps
Has no one any to give?
Imprisoned soul
Free, can you let it live?
my mind gone forever
Has someone an extra to spare?

—to spare me…

If you hear my words
why do you ignore my despair
do you have anything?
Anyone?
just anything to spare—

—to spare me.

## *Oath of Despair*

I am asleep.
Hidden…
Withdrawn from the world I've grown to loathe,
lost from those that once loved me.

I sit in their shadows,
watching them laugh,
and do as they do,
picking up on their whispers—
Their tales of yours truly.

I attend to the lies,
they swim in my intellect,
each attached to my mind like a tumor.

I sense the sins of these lies,
but I am not holy enough to rebuke them
back to hell where they belong.

These creatures grow bitter over me,
Grow bitter over their own deceptive lifestyles.

I am voiceless.
They're persistent to shatter me,
but what is broken, can break no more.

They desire to dispose of me.
I desire to run.
Six miles away would suit them fine.
Six feet under would suit me well.
Asleep…
And hidden…
Just as I am now.

## Over My Head

Resting,
watching the clouds slip by,
as I write words come to me,
to set my soul free.

Examining constellations,
of these damned nations,
interpreting my songs,
set to rectify of my wrong.

I plummet into desolation,
bringing forth a revelation,
wading through an outline of faith,
set to find my place.

## *Past, Present, Death*

Fighting the world happenings,
begging to be reborn,
wanting to start over,
erase my mortal sins,
leaving me pure and untainted,
amnesia would be my cure,
watching the bruises slowly fade,
healing the scars,
removing the bandages,
Plagued with knowledge,
becoming a self titled novel.
Broken and bending.
Twisted in binding.
What shall bring release?
Cursing my demons away,
speaking of freedom,
preaching from passion
Pure, distinct in all my glory
Death will be my only perfection
—the only present.

## *Pure as Gold*

Colored by sins,
yet still see pure.
How clean is pure?
How pure is gold?
What's the meaning that held in your palms?
What's the song, sung aloud,
if nothing more than a simple pleasure?
If that's true, then what's false?
If truth is pure, then what's gold?
No single thing can be more,
unless perhaps combined with another.
What if you separated them,
would they hold a stain from past?
Sinners are we.
Yet forgiven also.
For finest gold is tainted,
as we.
Simple in impurity.
Thus I will continue to sing.
Perhaps, I will never know the purpose of my voice,
but it pleases me nonetheless.

## *Rebirth*

A rose stained cheek,
of the damsel that resides within,
how lovely her heart,
how fair her beauty,
resting in a meadow of feathers,
observing cascading sunsets,
while little cherubs,
dance around with syrupy chants,
their giggles make her smile…

Life is witnessed,
like a rose stained cheek,
her creation is born,
A longing, released.

At last,
the birth of her.

## *Resting Mind*

I'm tired of making out the figures drawn within my head,
my mind is bewildered,
thoughts have expanded,
And heart seems, oh so dead.

Feels like I haven't a thing to hold onto, for this 'thing' isn't my place.
I close my eyes
to fly away
and dance upon my grace.

Wherever this feeling…
Wherever this thought…
is confusing the choices I've made.

I wish to return
to the place of my dwelling—
the place where I once laid.

# Riddance Fortune

Words are scripted,
beliefs are hollow,
speaking in riddles,
he thinks, I'll follow.

Mind is transparent,
Love has built a wall
holding onto nothing,
he expects, I'll fall.

Steps are backwards,
guidance has failed,
though diminishing slowly,
He hopes to prevail.

Yet to see him cry,
apt a cruel landing,
a plummet from riches,
when he's no longer standing.

## *Rily*

Dear Rily,
How ya doin',
Whats the news,
And where ya goin'?
Been a long time,
since we've spoken
heard your heart's been,
deeply broken?

Dear Rily,
Love the hair style,
Hope you soon,
get back your sweet smile,
though the stresses,
seem to pile,
I'd love to hang out,
for a while.

Never know when your next
adventure's starting,
pressing on the past
is slowly parting,
just give your all,

and hope it comes back to you,
And if you lose it all,
Remember,
I do, Rily I do.

Dear Rily,
Got your letter,
heard things were
gettin' better.
Found a pathway
to your liking,
hope it gives you
all the right things.

Dear Rily,
What's happenin'
Leavin' myself
fully open.
Just be kind
with what you know
and kiss me once
before you go.

So selfishly, I pray,
That you'll love me too, someday.
Daydreaming of a time,

when we'll make true of my rhyme,
but if I find my wishes,
don't come true,
Please remember,
Rily, I do…
Rily I do…

## *Runaway*

Where do you run to
when your past follows
your memories committed
though you can't admit it
spinning round and round
fixated on your thoughts?

Where do you turn
when your pain consumes you,
every step forward,
seems like the wrong direction?

How do you change?
How would you feel?
Is it sorrow or pity?
Is it anything more than your own delusions?

When the walls cave in
showing how weak you are,
would you die?
…Have I?

## Secret Love

I sit in my room and wait
for you, my love to be
I dream...
Day-dream...
Night-dream...
Visions twirling of you and me.
I pray for you,
think of you
Hold you...
mold you into me.
I watch you from my tower,
begging to be freed,
Wishing you'll want me.
I wait...
I dream...
I pray...
Someday my love...
Someday.
I want to know you, breath you, feel you,
Love you, kiss you,
If only,
I could see you.
If only,
If only, you knew.

## Set in Time

The beginning is to be the end…

When a dream lay upon his nest,
to keep his lonesome heart at rest,
he'll sleep alone into the night,
dreaming of lovers in sinful plight.

He weeps and sheds a hollow sigh,
soon recalling his midnight cries.
A darkened soul, bitter and bare,
as shadows leap from channeled despair.

The words were lost to battle tears,
his mind adorned in vanishing fears,
an unscripted song was a dreamer's rhyme,
to brand his story, a place in time.

The end has now begun…

## Shapeless

Blame it on the sun
rectify your soul
can you find the moon
placing you in role?

Silver grace betrays
somehow left unknown
sleepless in your mind
peaceful as it's shown.

Candle maker's dream
mold you day-to-day
can they not decide
leading you astray?

Ride upon your star
floating on a cloud
a love that is your high
can you find it now?

# Sir, No Sir!

Quit following me, sir.
I need you not.

Stop calling me, sir!

Please…

Please…

Let me be, sir.

Stop asking for my hand, sir.
I desire you not,
end this charade, now.

Mocking me…

Stalking me…

Move along, sir!

I require my space,
You're moving too close.

These lips are not yours, sir,
my heart is now free, sir.

Please…

Please…

Just let me be, sir!

## Sister Echo

In hard times, I feel alone,
sitting at the bottom of a dusty canyon,
imagining the river I no longer can see,
like the histories of life, what once used to be.

Whispering through the broken tears,
enraged, yet breathing still engulfed in fears,
feeling the blazing sand, scorching my days,
echoing my past, as it all replays.

Speak to me, sweet sister echo,
let the walls claim not your voice,
help me find an understanding,
as you paraphrase wisdom as choice.

Though a hollow tale you tell.

The sun is setting and I'm alone,
the cold walls are closing in,
I loathe these artistic vibes,
that only desolation revives.

In this capsulation of earthly shadows,
I seek my voice, but the world abandons me,
yet again, what could it provide,
by trying to hide, as it reminds me of her story?

Speak to me, sweet sister echo—
you're all that I have had,
you're all that I have left,
cry out all your passion.

Take in your last breath,
though hollow is the air you breathe,
only you can truly see,
the lasting words declared by me.

## *Solitude*

Mental suffocation
upon a revelation
of echoing taunts to break down.

Seedless reproducing
depression is seducing
breaking every fiber of my crown.

All the courts have adjourned
there is nothing I earned
except tease my unforgotten pain.

Doubtful in displacement
I must now reface him
there is nothing here that's left to gain.

## *Son*

Inside my womb
a freshly planted bloom
grows gracefully day by day.
As life gently lies
innocence ever pure
as coming months seem a blur.
Fear shivers my spine
happiness keeps me high.
I feel him move and dance
as though in a liquid trance.
He's cradled as I walk along
rests so deeply and calm.
Late nights begin
before meeting him.
I hear his heartbeat,
Slow, then fast
hoping pain would pass.
Finally cutting through my fear
The most beautiful song to hear
the sound of my angels' cry
needing mommy by his side.
The most precious gift I could receive
a baby boy, born from me.

## The Only Road I Know

Always running down,
the long road ahead,
life isn't fair for the living,
it is only fair for the dead.

Seems my life was spent well,
but well was spent long ago,
now I keep spiraling down,
the only road I know.

Trying to save my dreams,
as they cascade to the floor,
in a room without windows,
and one bolted door.

I tried forgetting everything,
love isn't what I need,
how could I possibly love,
while heart continues to bleed?

Yet I'll continue driving,
down endless road to nowhere,
and I look in the rearview mirror,
to find no one standing there.

## *The Orchestra*

Merry art thou roses bloom,
wretched is thy rain,
Painting thy hearts silhouette,
teacher rings thy name.

Noted for an orchestra,
bleed it's nothing more,
Chained in garnered memory,
your dreams, thy heart restores.

Listen chanted note and harp,
listen…listen here,
hold thy own painted tune,
of sea upon thy ear.

Let us come to-and-fro,
chic our clothing wear,
silk is thus thy harmony,
voices calm the air.

Go on passage great of clay,
talk and talk again,
the only song is of the sky,
essence of thy sin.

# The Scavenger

Dead limbs taunt the crimson tide,
vanquished, the lion's pride,
treasury found so deep and wide,
as the scavenger roves through the night.

Echoes stir a ransom fest,
the messenger begins his belated quest,
the fearsome lion mustn't rest,
as the scavenger roves through the night.

Cherubic dancers paint the sky,
the unbridled lion must fortify,
his every weakness and tired sigh,
as the scavenger roves through the night.

A feeble lamb sleeps through the day,
a marauder, the lion, consumes his prey,
swindle by a passing knave,
as the scavenger roves through the night.

The clouds relinquish their saddened rain,
graced as the moon reveals distain,
the lion feels the nights' chilled pain,
as the scavenger roves through the night.

Now hunted, the dormant lion hides,
behind his deepened shallow pride.
every wrong shall rectify,
as the scavenger roves through the night.

## *The Sparrow Song*

Like a sparrow,
as the raindrops fall
upon my weary eyes,
like the shadows,
that fall down,
upon my daunting cries,
I try too hard,
to reach for you,
but you never seem to be there,
and as I cry,
my heart will try,
to open up again,
when the sadness,
falls from the sky,
upon my misery,
strange and saddened,
are the hopeless dreams,
longing for those memories.

## The Sweetest Moment

The moment I saw you,
My life was complete,
when I heard your heart,
I counted every beat.

The moment I felt you,
for the first time,
I knew right then and there,
that you were to be mine.

The moment I heard your voice,
and the poetic beauty you sang,
was when my heart first throbbed,
faster and faster it rang.

The moment you kissed me,
I wanted it so much,
it was the moment I knew,
I would never leave your touch.

## The World I Live In

I live outside of your mortal brains,
deadly-alive I am,
I float in space without distain,
out here it's not so crammed.
You think, talk, and look alike,
you busy little bees.
Stubborn, dull, you walk on spikes,
your world makes me displeased.
In your senseless lasting haikus,
my misery is well graced.
You're knocked down and still continue,
my knowledge is displaced.
Always do you stare at me,
as though I have your need,
when in my world, I'm full of life,
with happy pain I bleed.

## *This Day*

This day is real,
though yesterday I cried,
consumed with sorrow and confusion.

Mortal on the edge,
that no time capsule could relieve.

This day is real,
Forget yesterday,
though tomorrow may be broken.

If pushed,
I'll stand again.
Should I cease to exist,
I'll reincarnate.

Forget tomorrow,
because this day is real,
and right now,
I am fine.

Content…

## *This Night*

Night is an epic—
Playing its beautiful songs,
as eons pass.
It has untold futures,
mischievous pasts.
Torments of the broken,
lovers of this night,
death becoming.
Sleepless hours,
slumbers of still,
cradles of passion,
mothers of will.
Night has a story—
As all did before,
all will again,
rectifying pasts,
creating new sins.
Daughter's creations,
son's magnificence,
sister's of the streets,
brother's malevolence.
Night tells tales—
Tales of yore—

Tales of us—
Tales to be told.

## *Traveler*

This was once native soil,
a place I once called home.
Now laying in ruins, damned,
I continue this journey alone.

Once a mighty legend,
always knowing where to stand,
now evicted, not quite equipped,
misplaced in fabled command.

Whisper to me, someone,
somewhere.
I will follow…
I will follow!
Dwell within new walls,
existing eternally in sweet serenity.

Perhaps a new bay eagerly awaits,
to summon my dwindling tide,
to face a new, reverie,
and again restore my pride.

## Turning World

A spring story,
across time,
a green summer,
gold wine.
Be it morning,
lay the moon,
Be it night,
stars bloom.
Rushing wind,
praying sky,
sunny day,
gloomy cry.
Like breath,
the world turns,
like love,
a star burns.
Colorful dance,
round and round,
sleepless hour,
restless ground.

## Un-choosing Choices

My heart says one thing,
instinct yells another.
Unable to come to terms with each other,
to make up my mind.
Heart is easily broken,
instincts are as well forgotten.
Which stands out more?
The caress of an endless drum,
the obsession of my decisions,
Mind…
Body…
Soul…
Thoughts, heartache, and instinct.
When they are of the same person,
is it possible to choose only one?
Stuck at the fork in the road,
Veer to left…
Stray to the right…
Or turn back around?
try to conclude why they seem so separate.
Unable to come to terms with each other,
…to make up my mind.

## *Unforgiven*

So awake to the dawn's musk,
know the pain of Hell in dusk.
An angel of beast and darkness will pay,
overwhelmed into spirit, thou art carried away.
Cursed shadows bleed to thy name,
garner the thoughts of loathing and shame.
Vexed and scorned, each burned at thy stake,
waiting for punition, for the inevitable will break.
Unforgiven are those who strum the harp,
the pain and agony...
that impales thy heart.

## Unspoken Secrets

Pleasure is my pain,
drowning 'neath the rain,
praying to my purpose,
entangled within us.
Intrigued to deny,
too involved not to hide.
I love the one who chooses me,
I please the one who cannot see.
Bowing vile temptress,
whom never should he trust,
a high, I despise,
I feel his wanting eyes.
Staring deep into my soul,
unable to let go,
could this love e'er forgive,
if let my dark lies live?

## *Untitled*

Never before
felt so raw
undefined
yet understood.
You adjourn me.
Is my trial
once outstanded
while saints
plunder to kneeling?
Hopes alone
felt malnourished.
E'er it stop
so pleased undone
collective
enchanting goodbyes?

## *Waiting*

Why won't he call?
Why won't he acknowledge me?
I've spent so much time
Waiting…
I'm lonely in all—
Pacing with my misery
A desperate hope, which is failing.
So much we could do,
so much he could do with me,
I never angered so easily,
When I'm losing touch.
"I've lost so damn much!"
I say to him, so playfully,
Should I stand—
Naked—
Baring all I have to give?
I seek him,
across a deep canyon
my echoes scream out,
so emptily.
Is it me, he wants to be with?
Should I just wait?
Or should I fall forth

collapsing in this agony?
Or is my patience testing me?
Why won't he call?
Why won't he acknowledge me?
I've spent so much damn time…
Waiting…

## *What If...*

Love was a passage—
you would be the way.
Love was the sun—
you would be the day.
Love was the wake—
you would be the sea.
Love was a place—
at home is where I'd be.
Love was tears—
I wish it to rain.
You were love itself—
then love I would surely gain.

What if?

## *What Say You?*

How could you?
Why would you?
How dare you?
What say you?

The dead...
The dead...
The death of my heart...

This woven token of ice-lain past,
the threads of fate,
in evering last.

Why would you?
How could you?
What say you?
What be you?

The peace...
The peace...
The place I shall seek...

These tears of yore.
frigid life.
The dread of future—
releasing in strife.

So gone now,
You are now.
How dare you?
How dare you?

The death…
The death…
the deceased you shall seek…

This demented enrichment
to you, I know not,
release you eternally,
no more you are caught.

## Wishing Widow

I refuse to be the wife of pain and chaos.
I demand to live my life as I will,
release torture inside the night of blindness,
hiding a guild of peace within my mind,
I may never awake from the absence at stake.
Should one never hope for new beginnings?
In clouds of chants,
prayers and rants,
may we all consume the fear that lives within us…

## *Woe*

In woe…
Such woe…
one forced to bestow.
How you carry, bitter-sweet cherries,
to thine lips of a foe.
Oh grace…
Such grace…
The wreckage you face.
To heal a wound,
this woe replace,
to trace what grace may know.

## *Yore Words*

I cope with the premonition,
of yore he once inspired.
Hated when I missed him,
revoking my desires.
When beaten at this game,
we traveled round in circles.
Whom never should he blame,
who's living in this world.
If ever one so faint,
appear amongst the light.
Blinded by my hate,
away he will take flight.
A yore I cannot fail,
a future is to tell.
When apt to write this tale,
too many times I fell.
He mustn't feel this pain,
with which I carry deep.
And on again distain,
having courage to stand and speak.

## Your Illusion

Just leave me alone,
let me fade away for a moment.
Take my thoughts,
sort them out so I can sleep.
Hold all the calls,
so I can set my soul free.
Run a bath,
let drown out my miseries.
It's hard to fight this life,
bearing the pounds,
of the fate against me.
I'm now an illusion,
I cause your delusion.
Unbroken, yet unspoken,
The world turns hazy as stars finally die.
Just go away,
take my unguided heart with you.
Make me a potion,
so I can magically disappear.
Lock the doors,
let me hide here in my comfort.
Get me some wine,
so I can drink away my addictions.

For its hard to feel anything,
anymore.
When the touch of my fingertips are washed away,
just let me cry out in pain.
You won't hear me anymore,
Maybe soon I'll be at peace,
and finally die…with the stars.

## Your Wonder

I mean forever,
before the words come to mind,
lying in bed,
wondering, if it's all a dream.

So surreal it seems,
that you can love me,
I pinch my arm,
'Ouch'
I *am* in love.

How magnificent…
Wondrous you are…
In awe with this love,
How can it be real?

A dream-like passion,
Drives desires for more,
My today is, you.
My eternity is, you.
At a moment's cue.
I will.
'I do!'
For only you.

## *Yours*

In the hours of darkness,
I find myself dreaming about you.
At last, as I close my eyes,
I find myself dancing in your arms.

Your love seems to find me,
no matter where I lose myself.
Your thoughts drift through me,
no matter where my soul sails.
You're always in my heart,
no matter where you are.
You're always in my mind,
me, you always seem to find.

When I find you in my dreams,
I feel you,
feeling me deep inside—
Holding you so close to my heart,
adorning beats of life.

Your love seems to know me,
though I don't, myself sometimes.
Your thoughts seem to catch me,

adrift with my lonely rhymes.
You're always in my thoughts,
singing me to my sweet dreams.
You're always in my mind,
Me, you always seem to find.

I may not understand,
but I'll always take your hand,
trust you…
need you…
just get you…
and me.